LSAT PREP TEST 86

Logical Reasoning
Answer Explanations

Produced By

lsatmax

COMPREHENSIVE LSAT PREP ON
MOBILE & WEB

lsatmax.io/86

Claim your Free 30-Min LSAT Consultation

Ensure a strong start to your LSAT prep. Schedule your free LSAT consultation with a *99th percentile instructor*.

To Redeem Visit
lsatmax.io/consult-86

Try The #1-Rated LSAT Prep for Free.

⚡ **Instant & Lifetime Access**

📈 **Detailed Analytics**

📄 **90 Full Length LSATs**

🕐 **Weekly Office Hours**

％ **99th Percentile Instructors**

🏅 **Higher Score Guarantee**

📱 **Authentic Digital LSAT/ LSAT-Flex Experience**

🏆 **#1 for 3 Years in a Row**

lsatmax↗

COMPREHENSIVE LSAT PREP ON
MOBILE & WEB

Get 10% Off When You Enroll.

Kyle Ryman
Texas A&M

I scored below a 150 on my first practice LSAT in November. **In June I took the LSAT and scored a 170. I couldn't have done it without LSATMax.**

Anita Yandle
University of Washington

The tutorials from LSATMax helped me get my 99th percentile score! It was great to have the videos at my fingertips at all times so that I could study any time I had a moment.

Austin Sheehy
University of Central Oklahoma

LSATMax is my hero! **My starting score was around a 155-158, and I scored a 170 on the June LSAT!**

Naader Banki
USC

I used LSATMax to study for the October LSAT. **I started out with a diagnostic somewhere in the 150s, and improved my score to 166 on the October test.**

To Redeem Visit lsatmax.io/86 or Call (855) 464-9890

THE LEGAL LEVEL PODCAST

From the LSAT to the bar exam, we are leveling the legal education playing field by providing the tools and information every future lawyer needs to ace the LSAT, rock law school admissions, pass the bar exam and land their dream job.

Available wherever you listen to podcasts. Search for *The Legal Level*.

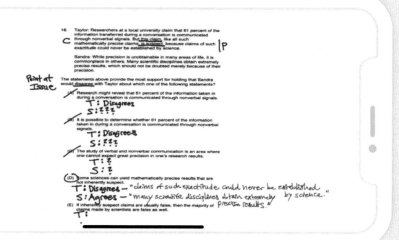

$\boxed{1}$

PT 86 - LR 1
QUESTION EXPLANATIONS

25 QUESTIONS

In this section we look at each LR question in depth by examining the stimulus, answer anticipation and each answer choice.

Q1

Argument or Facts: **Argument**
Valid or Flawed: **Flawed**
Question Type: **Strengthen**

Stimulus Summary:

Some apes eat more shrubbery during the rainy season. The author's explanation? The shrub's medicinal properties, since it helps eliminate worms. Gross way to start out the section, LSAT.

Answer Anticipation:

The conclusion talks about the medicinal properties of the leaves, which is established in the final clause, so that connection is unlikely to factor into correct answer. Instead, we should focus on the first premise. Why are the apes eating more during the rainy season? If we want to strengthen this argument, we should connect that season to the need for medicine to eliminate worms.

Correct Answer: (E)

Answer Choice Explanations:

A. If we were trying to strengthen an argument about whether these leaves have a certain effect, then this would be a great answer—it'd rule out an alternative possibility. However, the argument establishes that the leaves have the desired effect. Instead, we need to find an answer that connects the time the apes are eating them to that effect.

B. While we know chimpanzees are related to bonobos, we don't know if they're similar in gastrointestinal constitution. One ape's medicine might be another's poison! Additionally, the conclusion of this argument focuses on a specific shrub, not rough-surfaced leaves generally.

C. If anything, this weakens the argument by suggesting that the apes don't eat these leaves because they're medicinal, but rather because they're easy to find. It provides an alternative explanation for the behavior. Additionally, it's not tied specifically to the rainy season.

D. If anything, this weakens the argument by suggesting an alternative explanation for the increased leaf consumption during the rainy season. The bonobos aren't eating the leaves because they're medicinal, but rather because they're easier to eat. That said, this answer just mentions that they're *easier* to eat during the rainy season, not that they're easy to eat. Dirt is easier to eat with some ketchup on top, but that doesn't mean we're going to put it on the menu.

E. Exactly what we were looking for! This answer ties the rainy season to the need for medicine. If the bonobos tend to get stomach worms during the rainy season, it increases the likelihood that they're eating worm medicine to make themselves feel better.

Key Takeaway:

For a Strengthen question where the answer choice serves as an explanation for a phenomenon, anything that provides an alternative explanation serves as a weakener and can be eliminated (in a Weaken question, it'd be correct). Instead, focus on connecting facts from the premises to the explanation.especially an opinion of the counterpoint—it's almost certainly the main point of the argument.

Q2

Argument or Facts:	Argument
Valid or Flawed:	Flawed
Question Type:	Main Point

Stimulus Summary:

There are a bunch of ways to reduce traffic accidents. The author believes the best is to get people to drive less.

Answer Anticipation:

That "but" tells us a shift is happening. Usually, this shift is from the counterpoint to the author's argument. Here, the language following "but" suggests it's the conclusion. It is a prediction, an opinion, and a recommendation, all wrapped into one, and each of those tends to be a conclusion. The final sentence starts with, "The fact..." strongly suggesting it's a premise, so we should look for the second-to-last sentence in the answer choices.

Correct Answer: (D)

Answer Choice Explanations:

A. This statement isn't explicitly stated anywhere in the argument. It's more of an underlying principle.
B. The author's conclusion isn't about what another group should focus on; rather, it's about what would have the biggest impact. This statement also isn't stated in the argument.
C. This is a belief of the counterpoint, not a premise, and so it isn't explicitly stated in the argument. Additionally, if anything, it's a part of the counterpoint.
D. Correct! They tried to distract you by switching the "most" to "more than any other method," but those are logically equivalent.
E. This statement serves as the author's premise. The introductory phrase, "The fact is that..." is a great indicator you're dealing with a premise.

Key Takeaway:

Pivot words tend to indicate a shift from a counterpoint to the author's argument. If the statement that follows the pivot is a prediction, recommendation, or opinion—especially an opinion of the counterpoint—it's almost certainly the main point of the argument.

Q3

Argument or Facts:	**Argument**
Valid or Flawed:	**Flawed**
Question Type:	**Weaken**

Stimulus Summary:

The author accuses a newspaper of bias towards movies and against plays because of the relative frequency of reviews of the former versus the latter.

Answer Anticipation:

When the author of an argument settles on an explanation for a phenomenon, it's worthwhile to think about other possible explanations. Sure, more reviews of movies could mean a bias, but it could also mean that there are more movies to review, or a budget that only allows the reviewer to attend a few plays versus many more movies. Additionally, any argument that mentions frequency ("fives times as many") should consider the total number of occurrences. The focus on frequency here suggests that the first of our alternative explanations is likely to be the correct answer, since it deals with the total number of occurrences.

Correct Answer: (B)

Answer Choice Explanations:

A. This answer choice is trying to get you to think that the newspaper in question is better than other newspapers, since it publishes at least some reviews of plays. However, we don't know if these other newspapers even post reviews, thus making them a bad point of comparison! And even if this newspaper is less biased than others, it could still be biased.

B. This answer gets at the frequency explanation. It weakens the author's explanation that the more frequent movie reviews is due to bias by suggesting it's due to more frequent movie releases.

C. Well played, LSAT. This is a tempting trap answer. One might think that more movie reviewers serves as an alternative explanation for more movie reviews. However, having hired five movie reviewers by itself might suggest a bias, so this answer doesn't put forward an explanation that is at odds with the author's, and thus it doesn't weaken the conclusion.

D. Great, so there's not enough room to review everything. This doesn't affect the author's view that, with the limited space available, the newspaper doesn't display bias by selecting primarily movies to review over plays.

E. Even if the newspaper is less biased towards movies this year by including more reviews of plays, it doesn't mean that it doesn't still display a lamentable amount of bias against plays overall. Also, reviewing more plays doesn't mean that the ratio of movies to plays has decreased—maybe the ratio has always been 5:1, and they reviewed fewer plays in previous years.

Key Takeaway:

When the author provides an explanation for a phenomenon in a Weaken question, look for alternative explanations. When the argument deals with frequency, looks for answers that deal with the total overall number of occurrences. That frequency vs. total error in reasoning (also often seen as percents vs. amounts) recurs.

Q4

Argument or Facts:	**Argument**
Valid or Flawed:	**Flawed**
Question Type:	**Main Point**

Stimulus Summary:

There are some artifacts. They belong in a museum! Just not this one, possibly. There's a "rule" that artifacts belong where they're discovered, and the museum is obligated to follow that rule, these artifacts in the museum should be returned.

Answer Anticipation:

"Should" is a great conclusion indicator word. Unless a "should"-based principle is given and then applied, deriving an alternative conclusion, a statement with "should" in it is almost always the conclusion. Here, the rest of the statements also build to that final determination that the museum should return the artifacts.

Correct Answer: (A)

Answer Choice Explanations:

A. Exactly what we were looking for.
B. Much better. If the predator drops a possum that's This is a premise/principle that the argument applies to arrive at its conclusion.
C. This statement is a slight term shift from one given in the argument ("were obtained" vs. having documentation showing it). A good sign that a statement isn't the main conclusion is that it starts with "Although," since the author is going to pivot away from that contention.
D. This is the background of the entire situation.
E. An expanded version of (B), and wrong for the same reason.

Key Takeaway:

"Should" is a key indicator of a conclusion. There are times when it will show up outside of a conclusion, but those are relatively rare.

Q5

Stimulus Summary:

Prediction accurate/Precognitive -> Predicted event happens

Some predicted events don't happen.

Therefore, often not precognitive.

Answer Anticipation:

Necessary Assumption questions with conditional logic have been rare historically, but they've been more common in recent years. Here, we are presented with a conditional rule, and the premise deals with the trigger of the contrapositive.

Whenever a single conditional rule is relied on to reach a conclusion, it's important to make sure that the premise that triggers it matches the sufficient condition given. Here, the condition is that the predicted events don't happen. However, premise is just that they *sometimes* don't happen. That switch in degree is something that has to be bridged for the argument to work.

Correct Answer: (A)

Answer Choice Explanations:

A. Exactly the connection we were looking for. Note that this answer would also serve as the correct answer to a Sufficient Assumption question.
B. First off, this answer is about people, not characters in books. Big difference. Second, this answer overshoots what's needed for the argument to work. The conclusion is just that these characters are *often* not truly precognitive, not that they always lack precognition.
C. The argument relies on the established premise that some of these works do feature predictions that don't happen. Also, it would be difficult for an answer that leaves a question open to be necessary to reach a conclusion relying on something not happening.
D. The argument just cares about whether the characters have precognitive abilities, not how much that matters to the plot.
E. This answer also overshoots the argument. The conclusion given is just that these works often lack truly precognitive characters; this answer goes past that to stating they never feature truly precognitive characters.

Key Takeaway:

For any argument that relies on the triggering of a single conditional statement, check to be sure that the premise triggering it matches with the actual condition. The LSAT will often feature a term shift here that can lead you to the answer. Also, for Necessary Assumption questions, be sure that you don't select an answer overshooting the conclusion.

Stimulus Summary:

Unemployment is up, so it's no shock that injuries are down. However, it is shocking that the percent of workers injured is down.

Answer Anticipation:

Without knowledge of what has happened in a workplace other than there being fewer workers, there's no reason to expect the workplace to get safer. Here, however, it did. Any answer that puts forward an explanation for why the workplaces became safer resolves this paradox, so those answers should be eliminated.

We can specifically anticipate an answer about fewer people in the workplace making it safer. Especially if you work in an open office...

Correct Answer: (D)

Answer Choice Explanations:

A. If someone is working fewer hours, there's less time for them to get injured, so a decrease in injuries would be expected. This answer is similar to answers in questions on the LSAT about car safety, where less time on the road would be expected to lead to fewer accidents.

B. If workers are less pressured to hit a deadline, they have more ability to focus on safety. Anyone who's been behind on a deadline knows that your behavior gets riskier. And if that's not you, you'll experience it soon enough in law school!

C. This doesn't tell us anything about why the prey do engage in this behavior. It's just a neutral additional piece of information (common for wrong answers in this category).

D. This answer choice makes the paradox worse! If workplaces are spending less money on workplace safety, we'd expect to see an increase in injuries, not a decrease.

E. While not explicitly stated in the argument, we know that experienced workers are experienced, and thus more likely to know common sources of injury and how to avoid them. If the remaining workers are experienced, we'd expect injuries to go down.

Key Takeaway:

Common trap answers in Paradox questions provide information that makes the discrepancy worse, so in a Bizarro Paradox questions, those are commonly provided as correct answers.

Also, for Paradox questions, answers that resolve the paradox frequently rely on small, common-sense jumps. Here, we see this in answers (B) and (E), where the answer assumes that less pressure results in fewer accidents, and more experience leads to fewer accidents, respectively. While you can't make these jumps in other question types, those small jumps are generally acceptable in Paradox question.

Q7

Argument or Facts:	Argument
Valid or Flawed:	Flawed
Question Type:	Strengthen with Sufficient Premise

Stimulus Summary:

Appropriate for children → Not Threatening

Adult animated films have dark themes

Adult animated films not appropriate for children

Answer Anticipation:

A conditional rule is provided as a premise. Here, you'll note that we focused on "Not threatening" instead of "innocently whimsical" or "mischievous" because those are connected to that "perhaps" which means they're not guaranteed.

The conclusion is the negation of our sufficient condition, so we should take the contrapositive of the rule:

Threatening → Not appropriate for children

Now that our conclusion matches up with the necessary condition, we should check to see if the premise triggers that rule. Here, it doesn't. We're told that these adult animated films have dark themes, not that they're threatening. That must be the gap, so we should look for an answer stating:

If a film has dark themes, then it's threatening.

Correct Answer: (C)

Answer Choice Explanations:

A. This answer fails to connect what we know about the adult animated films to what we know about animated films appropriate for children. Without that connection, we can't get to the conclusion.

B. This answer choice undershoots the conclusion. The author concludes that these movies aren't appropriate for children, whereas this answer says they're seldom appropriate.

C. Exactly right. If films with dark themes are threatening, then we know these adult animated films are threatening. If they're threatening, according to the first premise, then they're not appropriate for children.

D. This answer doesn't get to the heart of the argument—whether the films are appropriate for children. Enjoyment doesn't factor into the argument.

E. If anything, this answer choice suggests that the films might be appropriate for children in that they might not pick up on those dark themes. If an answer in a Sufficient Assumption question could provide evidence against the conclusion, it can't be correct.

Key Takeaway:

When an argument relies on a single conditional being triggered, leading to the conclusion, make sure that the triggering premise matches that sufficient condition. Here, there's a gap between the given trigger ("threatening") and the premise the author uses to trigger it ("dark themes").

Argument or Facts: Argument
Valid or Flawed: Flawed
Question Type: Errors in Reasoning

Stimulus Summary:

Monarch butterflies have to deal with some gnarly parasites that stop them from migrating. Comparing non-migrating to migrating populations, we see that 95% of non-migrating monarchs are infected, compared to 15% of migrating monarchs. The author concludes that migrating allows monarch to avoid infection.

Answer Anticipation:

Any argument that relies on comparing two groups needs a deeper analysis of these two groups. Here, the author tells us that the groups are different—one has never migrated, the other migrates. So it seems as if migrating has something to do with the infection rate (though that's not guaranteed). But does it have to be what the author states?

Since this is an Errors in Reasoning question, no! There must be another explanation as to why we see this difference in parasite infection between the non-migrating and migrating group.

Knowing that is enough of an anticipation, but you could go a step further and think about some alternatives. One is that the author has it backwards—migrating doesn't cause safety from infection; infection causes the butterflies to not migrate. This makes sense since we've been told the parasites hurt the butterflies' ability to fly.

Correct Answer: (D)

Answer Choice Explanations:

A. Tempting answer. One might think that their inability to detect the parasites undermines the author's conclusion that migrating allows them to avoid the parasites. However, if the monarchs accidentally avoid the parasites through migrating, that works just as well for the argument as if they intentionally flee the areas with parasites.

B. Since the argument doesn't mention any length of migration, or connect the parasites to migration length, this answer choice is outside the scope of the argument.

C. The premise about relative infection rates deals with just that—rates. The number of butterflies in the populations doesn't impact the rate of infection. This jump between percent and overall amount is a common trap the LSAT will lay for you!

D. This answer gets at the reversal ignored by the author. It's not that migrating prevents infection, but rather that infection prevents migration.

E. Unless you're a lepidopterist (which may or may not be the correct term for butterfly scientist), you can't say whether the parasites are related to a food source. This answer choice suggests an alternative reason for the monarchs not to migrate, but it doesn't connect that to parasitical infection, and so it's outside the scope of the argument.

Key Takeaway:

When a conclusion settles on an explanation, consider alternative explanations. When a conclusion deals with causality, consider if the reverse makes sense. When an argument brings up percent, be careful of answers that deal with numbers or overall size.

Q9

Argument or Facts: **Argument**
Valid or Flawed: **Flawed**
Question Type: **Strengthen (Principle)**

Stimulus Summary:

Principle: Government appropriates private property → Offer fair compensation

Application: If the government diminishes property values through an action, then it must offer fair compensation.

Answer Anticipation:

Since the necessary conditions of the Principle and Application match here, we need to look at the sufficient conditions to see where the gap is. Here, the principle is about appropriating property, while the application is about diminishing property values. That gap must be bridged to justify the application, so we should look for an answer that connects diminishing property values to appropriating.

Correct Answer: (C)

Answer Choice Explanations:

A.   Jump out of this answer choice as soon as it says what the government "should not" do. The Principle/Application is about what the government must do, not what it should do. Additionally, this argument doesn't deal with other properties.

B.   This answer might justify government action to appropriate or not appropriate private land, but it doesn't speak to compensation.

C.   This answer matches our anticipation perfectly. If diminishing value is the same as appropriating, then the application of the principle holds.

D.   If anything, this answer choice would justify not compensating property owners after an appropriation, since the property owners are solely responsible for economic risks, including the risk of government seizure.

E.   Oh, Kelo. Dear reader, you'll know the beauties of this Supreme Court case soon enough. In the meantime, you don't need this knowledge to see this answer is wrong. The argument is not about whether the government can appropriate private land; it's about providing compensation when doing so.

Key Takeaway:

This is the third question in this section alone where the key gap was between the sufficient condition of a conditional premise, and another premise given by the author. This question was slightly different from the first two in that the gap was between the sufficient condition of two conditionals, rather than the sufficient condition and a triggering premise, but the same logic applies. This type of error in reasoning is very common, so be on the lookout for it whenever conditional logic is present.

Q10

Argument or Facts: **Facts**
Valid or Flawed: **N/A**
Question Type: **Argument Completion**

Stimulus Summary:

Birds must stabilize a lot of pressure to fly. The pressure must be balanced. The only thing that can balance it is this one ligament. Therefore...

Answer Anticipation:

It must be the ligament that balances the pressure and stabilizes the bird. For these Argument Completion questions, the conclusion almost always wraps up the argument by bringing all the premises together— don't expect to leave anything out or bring in any new information.

Correct Answer: (E)

Answer Choice Explanations:

A. While this argument tells us one requirement for flight (balancing certain forces), it doesn't establish that as the only requirement. Unless you're an ornithologist (yes, we're getting fancy with our science terms in these explanations), you have no means of analyzing this answer, so it can't complete this argument.

B. This answer reverses the "direction" of the argument. The ligament stabilizes the forces; it isn't what makes this stabilization necessary.

C. This is too strong. While we know that it's the only connection strong enough to balance the forces of flight, there may be other connections that serve other purposes.

D. Again, this reverses the "direction" of the argument. The ligament doesn't cause the forces; or, at least, it doesn't cause all of them. It balances those forces.

E. The bird must stabilize its wings, and this ligament is the only thing in town strong enough to do so. Therefore, it must be what does it.

Key Takeaway:

For Argument Completion questions, beware answers that bring up all the relevant ideas but in a way that doesn't "flow" with the argument itself.

Q11

Argument or Facts: **Argument**
Valid or Flawed: **Flawed**
Question Type: **Strengthen (Principle)**

Stimulus Summary:

In a new subway project, a majestic station can be built, or a more modest station can be built. The former would be over budget with a convenient tunnel; the latter wouldn't. Since the project can't be over budget, the modest station should be built.

Answer Anticipation:

This conclusion picks one option at the expense of another—the more modest station with a tunnel over the majestic station without it. When a conclusion makes a recommendation, the premises need to set up the criteria for the comparison, and then discuss how each station matches those criteria. Here, the comparison of the stations is made (majestic vs. modest; no tunnel vs. tunnel), but the criteria for selection are never established.

The correct answer, therefore, will establish the criteria. Here, the selection is being made based on the inclusion of the convenient tunnel, as opposed to the more majestic station.

Correct Answer: (C)

Answer Choice Explanations:

A. While the budget can't be increased, the proposed solution could come in at budget. We also aren't told if the modest station with the tunnel is under budget, which would be required for this to be the answer.

B. The conclusion here selects one option out of two presented. This answer is just about considering all options, which isn't enough to strengthen the conclusion selecting a given option.

C. This answer establishes convenience over majesty. That criteria is what was missing from the argument, and it allows the recommendation in the conclusion to hold, which strengthens the author's argument.

D. Abandon the station? That's coming out of nowhere. The author concludes that the budget for the station should be cut to make it more modest but free up money for a tunnel. At no point does she suggest this is the only solution, or that the transit authority should walk away from the project completely.

E. Comparing the subway renovation project to all other potential projects is outside the scope of the argument.

Key Takeaway:

When an argument makes a recommendation in the conclusion, check to see if the author has established the criteria by which solutions will be judged. If she hasn't, then the correct answer will usually do just that.

Q12

Stimulus Summary:

Since doctors diagnose more left-brain strokes, it's likely that right-brain strokes are more likely to go undiagnosed.

Answer Anticipation:

Undiagnosed? Where'd that come from? Why can't it be that more strokes happen in the left side of the brain than the right side?

The author fails to rule out the possibility that more strokes occur in the left side of the brain than the right side. To strengthen this argument, the correct answer will probably do so, either by stating the number of strokes in both sides of the brain should be relatively even, or more strokes are expected to occur in the right side of the brain than the left side.

Correct Answer: (B)

Answer Choice Explanations:

A. This answer does nothing to explain the discrepancy in left- and right-brain strokes, or the frequency of diagnosing them. As far as we know, other health problems have nothing to do with strokes of either side of the brain.

B. While not definitive ("very likely"), it does increase the likelihood that strokes occur relatively evenly in both sides of the brain. If that's the case, and more left-brain strokes are diagnosed, it strengthens the conclusion that the right-brain strokes frequently go undiagnosed.

C. While this answer might appear tempting by suggesting a reason that some strokes go undiagnosed, it doesn't explain why those diagnoses skew towards one side of the brain. Presumably, the doctors good at diagnosing strokes would see just as many patients with left-brain strokes as right-brain ones.

D. A common trap answer! If it had stated that the right-brain stroke symptoms are harder to notice than those of left-brain strokes, then we'd have an answer. But since the answer is neutral—it just says they're different—this doesn't strengthen the argument.

E. Another answer that would be correct with an additional piece of information. If this answer stated that right-brain strokes were more likely to be minor strokes, then this would strengthen the argument. However, since it doesn't connect minor strokes to either side of the brain, it doesn't impact the argument.

Key Takeaway:

If an answer choice is neutral, or, in other words, if different ways of interpreting it would change it from being a correct to an incorrect answer, it can be eliminated in Strengthen and Weaken questions (but not Argument Evaluation questions). Here, for example, the answer stating that the symptoms are different requires an additional statement to know what impact it has on the argument. If right-brain stroke symptoms are harder to diagnose than left-brain stroke symptoms, then the answer has a different impact on the argument than if they're easier to diagnose.

Q13

Stimulus Summary:

A bunch of oysters died, to the point where some almost went extinct. The cause was initially and wrongly assumed to be temperature, but later proved to be this chemical TBT. TBT was banned, but some of the oysters didn't come back.

Answer Anticipation:

If something causing an animal to die off is removed, we'd expect the animal to stop dying. Here, that didn't happen, so we need to look for an answer that explains why the oysters didn't come back.

While there are several reasons, brainstorming a few quickly before heading to the answers can sometimes help. Maybe TBT stays in the environment for a long time, even after more stops being added. Maybe the oysters learned that this area was deadly and moved on to another area (smart oysters).

Correct Answer: (C)

Answer Choice Explanations:

A. Since the author states that warming water ended up not being the cause of the die-off, mentioning that the warming slowed in recent years doesn't help explain why these oysters didn't come back. Additionally, note that this answer says it slowed, not that it stopped or reversed—the water is still getting warmer.

B. If this is true, then whether barnacles are on the hulls of ships is immaterial to the number of oysters we'd expect to see, and thus this answer doesn't present information that's relevant to the paradox.

C. Very interesting answers that brings a lot of information together! The first suspected cause—warmer temperature—ends up relevant here, even though we might not have expected that. However, if other types of oysters that crowd out the endangered ones are now thriving, that would explain why the endangered ones didn't come back. This didn't match one of our anticipated answers (maybe it matched one of yours, in which case, great job). Stay flexible!

D. First, this answer assumes that these other chemicals are now used on boats off the coast of Britain, which may not be true. Second, even if we assume these other chemicals are in use, it doesn't explain why no change in the population occurred. With "safe" chemicals in use, the population should have rebounded.

E. If anything, this makes the paradox worse by suggesting the warming water should have resulted in the population being less affected by TBT over the years, instead of going nearly extinct and not rebounding. However, this answer really doesn't do anything for the paradox, since we know that TBT is no longer in use.

Key Takeaway:

The correct answer in a Paradox question will frequently not match with your anticipated answers. Stay flexible! And rely more on your generic idea of what you're looking for rather than any specific version of that. Here, we brainstormed a few specific ideas, but the key to finding the correct answer was to focus on our generic anticipation—an explanation for why the oysters didn't rebound in population after TBT was banned.

Q14

Argument or Facts:	Argument
Valid or Flawed:	Flawed
Question Type:	Weaken

Stimulus Summary:

People almost always get rabies from animal bites. Bats have rabies. But they're shy, and very few have rabies, so there's no need to warn people to deal with a bat infestation.

Answer Anticipation:

Definitely a question written by Bruce Wayne.

For many Weaken questions, it can be helpful to think about strengthening the opposite of the author's conclusion in order to weaken it. Here, even if bats are shy and don't generally have rabies, why might it still be a good idea to warn people about the health risks of living with bats? (This shouldn't be a tough question!)

Maybe there's something about rabid bats that make them different from normal bats—they are rabid, after all. Even if they're rare, if rabid bats are not shy, then there should probably be warnings against living with them.

Unless you're a billionaire with a vendetta.

Correct Answer: (B)

Answer Choice Explanations:

A. If anything, this suggests that bats aren't a threat to humans, thus working in favor of the author's conclusion.
B. A classic misdirect at the beginning of this answer! A lack of mobility might suggest rabid bats are safer, but the second half states that they're much more aggressive. If this is the case, the author's premise that they're shy is less relevant to the discussion of rabid bats, and thus the conclusion is weakened.

C. This answer is trying to trap you into picking it by making you think that bats are like other animals when not rabid, so maybe they're similar to other animals when rabid, and thus public health warnings are warranted. However, since the argument doesn't establish that public health warnings are warranted for other species, this answer choice is missing a key piece of information.
D. This answer includes relative language—"highest incidence." Maybe, however, those bat species have only a slightly higher incidence of rabies than other bat species that do tend to live in, say, caves hidden under mansions. In any case, this answer suggests that the warnings aren't necessary, and thus has, if anything, a strengthening impact on the argument.
E. When the bat bites, it's already too late, and that person has rabies. Whether it's easy to notice you've been bitten doesn't help you avoid the bite in the first place. Which is a bad thing—spider bites give you super powers, not bat bites.

Key Takeaway:

A lot of these answers fall into common patterns. The right answer has a misdirection in the beginning. One wrong answer includes relative language that isn't strong enough to weaken the argument (D). Another has a small jump based on what one might expect based on knowledge from the real world (C). Knowing these common trap answers and misdirects can make it easier to eliminate trap answers while avoiding eliminating correct answers.

Q15

Stimulus Summary:

Complete understanding leads to forgiveness. You can never completely understand yourself, so you can never forgive yourself. (We assume that you're trying to forgive yourself for skipping your last study session. For shame.)

Answer Anticipation:

When we simplify this argument, we can see that this falls into one of the most common flaws on the exam—illegally negating a statement. While complete understanding leads to forgiveness, the argument never establishes it as the only way to get forgiveness. However, the rest of the argument treats it that way.

We should look for an answer that points out there may be other things that lead to forgiveness.

Correct Answer: (A)

Answer Choice Explanations:

A. For answers that use abstract language, try to rephrase them using the language from the argument. This answer can be rephrased as: treats the failure to completely understand yourself (which brings about forgiveness) as the only way to bring about forgiveness. And that's what we were looking for.

B. While this answer uses sufficient and necessary language, it's actually getting at a different flaw—a causal one. The first half of the answer talks conditional language, which is a correlation. The second half uses causal language—"results from." While jumping between correlative/conditional language and causal language is a flaw, it's not the one committed here.

C. This answer, similar to (B), does describe an error in reasoning that occurs on the LSAT. And this argument even includes language that is associated with this error—it starts with "It has been said." However, the conclusion starts with "If so," which let's us know the conclusion recognizes the premise might just be something people say, and not something that's true. Without that "If so," this is a correct answer.

D. The argument only deals with whether the goal is attainable, not whether it is desirable. This answer would be potentially correct if the argument made a judgment as to the value of this lack of self-forgiveness.

E. The argument is not about whether or not one should try to attain self-forgiveness; just whether it's possible to do so.

Key Takeaway:

When an Errors in Reasoning question has these abstract answer choices that don't mention the specific ideas in the argument, it's a good idea to try to substitute in the language from the argument to make them easier to understand. Also, these abstract answers frequently describe errors in reasoning present on the exam, just not in that specific question, so it's worth spending time learning what they mean.

Q16

Stimulus Summary:

A Jackson Pollock looks like something a child could draw, according to many. However, in a study, people shown the work of a child and the work of an abstract expressionist artist consistently picked the latter as more aesthetically pleasing, thus proving these works are aesthetically pleasing.

Answer Anticipation:

This argument has key language suggesting a specific error in reasoning—mainly, it jumps from "aesthetically better" to "aesthetically pleasing." Whenever an argument jumps from a relative term to an absolute one (better to pleasing), there's a good chance the correct answer will deal with this jump.

In this case, in order to reach the conclusion that the "better" works are actually aesthetically pleasing, we need to know that the art they're being compared to is also aesthetically pleasing. To think of a similar situation, if food A is tastier than food B, we don't know that food A is tasty. But if food A is tastier than food B, and food B is pretty tasty, we know food A is also tasty.

Correct Answer: (B)

Answer Choice Explanations:

A. This answer establishes that the judgments made are more accurate , but it doesn't let us know if these pieces of art are aesthetically pleasing.

B. Oh, LSAT, using double negatives to confuse us. If the preschoolers' paintings weren't displeasing, then they were either pleasing or neutral. In either case, this allows "better" to equate to "good." If the works of the preschoolers' were displeasing, then being better than them wouldn't guarantee any level of quality.

C. If anything, this calls the whole study into question. Knowing which paintings were which may have skewed the study, thus not allowing any conclusions to be validly drawn.

D. This answer tells us that there was some consistency in the ratings of the abstract expressionist paintings as better, even for those who didn't like them as frequently as the average. However, it still doesn't resolve the error in reasoning of the argument, as everyone could have hated all the paintings, and just hated the professional ones less.

E. The similarities in style, again, doesn't resolve the error between liking something better and finding it aesthetically pleasing.

Key Takeaway:

A common error in reasoning sees the author jump from relative language to absolute language (or vice versa), so be on the lookout for it.

Q17

Stimulus Summary:

X: It's not surprising the new McKingdy's went out of business since it only had outdoor seating, requiring diners to breath in exhaust fumes.

M: An outdoor-seating only fast food joint was likely to fail, so it was irresponsible to lend them money.

Answer Anticipation:

They both seems to agree that the new food place lacked indoor seating, and it was a bad idea.

Correct Answer: (E)

Answer Choice Explanations:

A. Xavier is closest to agreeing with this, but we don't know his opinion on outdoor seating that's away from a street with heavy traffic. Miranda states that outdoor-only seating is a bad idea, but she may be basing that more on choice than on the preference of most people. Neither clearly has an opinion on this answer, so they can't agree on it.

B. Xavier doesn't talk about banks at all, so this answer can be eliminated on that front alone. Miranda talks about banks, but she ties her criticism into the amount of competition, so we can't commit her to agreeing with this answer choice, either.

C. While both Xavier and Miranda tie their criticism of the new fast food joint to the seating, they may have other reasons to believe the restaurant was likely to fail, so we can't commit either to having an opinion on this answer.

D. Both tie their criticism to the exclusivity of outdoor seating, not having some outdoor seating. Another answer where neither of the speaker's has a clear opinion.

E. Xavier wasn't surprised that the restaurant failed. Miranda thinks it was irresponsible to lend money to the venture. Both of those statements are strong enough to support the contention that they found it to be risky.

Key Takeaway:

For Point of Agreement (and Point at Issue) questions, incorrect answers will frequently bring up ideas that neither speaker has a clear opinion on (or, only one of the speakers does). If it's not guaranteed that a speaker has an opinion on an answer, that answer can be safely eliminated.

Q18

Argument or Facts:	Facts
Valid or Flawed:	N/A
Question Type:	Paradox

Stimulus Summary:

This one type of bird sets up nests in woody vegetation, wooden boxes, and open areas at about the same frequency. Some birds reuse other birds' nests. One might expect them to reuse the woody vegetation nests, but they mostly use the box nests.

Answer Anticipation:

This paradox question presents three options (vegetation, boxes, and open), but only talks about two (vegetation and boxes). Our first anticipation is that open-area nests will not feature into the explanation, since they're not part of the paradox.

Focusing on the vegetation and box options, we should be open to any answer that explains why the vegetation nests wouldn't be used or the box ones would.

Correct Answer: (B)

Answer Choice Explanations:

A. This answer doesn't explain why the birds reuse box nests instead of vegetation nests; it doesn't even mention them.

B. This answer explains why the vegetation nests aren't used—they're hard to find. While we wouldn't select it on a first pass as it'd be better if it mentioned that the box nests are easier to find, it will end up being correct.

C. This answer doesn't state that the birds for vegetation nests behave more aggressively than those in box nests. Since it doesn't distinguish between the two, it can't explain why one type of nest is selected more than another.

D. This answer brings up a fact that would apply equally to both vegetation and box nests, so it doesn't explain the discrepancy in reuse between them.

E. This answer explains why the birds want to hide their nests, but not why they'd reuse the box nests more than the vegetation nests. If anything, this explains why they wouldn't choose the open nests, but that's not a part of the presented paradox.

Key Takeaway:

When the paradox in a Paradox question compares two options, answers that apply equally to both options won't resolve the paradox.

Q19

Argument or Facts: **Argument**
Valid or Flawed: **Flawed**
Question Type: **Errors in Reasoning**

Stimulus Summary:

Two similar groups were selected for an experiment. The only known difference is that the first group was given a medical self-help book; that group saw a doctor less. Since healthy people go to the doctor less, the book must have made people healthier.

Answer Anticipation:

This argument is dealing with a jump between correlation and causation, but there's a wrinkle in this question compared to most correlation/causation questions.

Usually, the premises are correlative, and the conclusion is causal. That's true of this argument, but there's *also* a causal premise, stating that good health leads to fewer doctor visits.

Normally, we'd expect an answer that points out the correlation/causation flaw. However, since this argument adds a causal premise, there's a good chance that's going to tie into the correct answer, possible stating that this explanation for how the self-help book decreased medical visits isn't related to good health, but rather some other explanation.

Correct Answer: (D)

Answer Choice Explanations:

A. While this is a possibility, it's not a possibility that impacts the argument. The first group definitely had the self-help book, whereas the second group only might have bought the book on their own. Statistically, the first group will have more families with the self-help book.

B. While this is a possibility, it's not a possibility that impacts the argument. The first group definitely had a self-help book, whereas the second group only might have accessed medical self-help information. Statistically, the first group will have more families with relevant information.

C. While this answer choice plays into the correlation/causation error in reasoning, it doesn't match with the argument. The argument doesn't treat a given cause as if it only has one effect. Rather, it treats two potential causes—the book and good health—as being related to each other.

D. Unlike (C), this answer deals with multiple potential causes. The argument conflates a decrease in doctor visits because of self-treatment and because of being healthier. Rephrasing this answer, it would state that both self-treatment and good health contribute to fewer doctor visits without either causing the other. In other words, the self-help book might have decreased doctor visits through a method other than making people healthier.

E. This answer reverses the connection, stating that a state of affairs (such as being healthier) could lead to having a self-help book. The argument assumes just the opposite of that. Additionally, we know that the families in the study were given this book, so an answer that deals with families buying it on their own is out of scope.

Key Takeaway:

Correlation/causation errors in reasoning are some of the most frequent errors tested on the LSAT. Here, they add a relatively rare wrinkle by adding in a causal premise, but if you're strong on the foundations, you can adapt when the writers change things up.

Q20

Argument or Facts: **Argument**
Valid or Flawed: **Flawed**
Question Type: **Strengthen (Principle)**

Stimulus Summary:

Political pressure leads to inaccuracies in government reports, so these ministries shouldn't issue scientific reports.

Answer Anticipation:

Strengthen (Principle) questions will frequently break down to connecting the simplified premise to the conclusion. Here, we learn that these scientific assessments are politically biased. The author concludes, then, that they shouldn't be issued.

The correct answer will most likely connect those: If a government ministry would release an inaccurate scientific report because of political pressure, then it shouldn't issue that report.

Correct Answer: (B)

Answer Choice Explanations:

A. The argument is about accuracy and whether the reports should be issued, not whether there's a need for them. Additionally, the argument never states whether these health reports are necessary. Sure, they haven't existed, but that could have been a major problem for the government in that it was missing necessary information.
B. Rephrasing this to simplify the complex conditional language ("unless"), this breaks down to: If a ministry doesn't have a strong reason to believe it can release an accurate report, it shouldn't issue the report. This matches our prephrase and the argument. The correct answer to this question type can often feel as if you're mostly restating the argument!
C. The argument itself doesn't judge whether the political pressure is a bad thing; just that it exists and should preclude the release of reports.
D. This is a tempting answer, but it's the inverse of what the argument assumes. This answer would justify a conclusion about what the government should do, not what it shouldn't do, as we see in this argument.
E. This argument is about whether the ministry should issue a report, not whether it should resist the pressure. While you may think the author takes a negative opinion of that pressure, and that the ministries should thus fight back, it's not what the argument itself is about.

Key Takeaway:

Strengthen (Principle) questions frequently have correct answers that sound very repetitive of the argument itself.

Q21

Stimulus Summary:

Farming with chemicals hurts the environment, but it lets you grow more food. Organic farming is better for the environment, but if everyone did it, people would starve. Let's stop the spread of organic farming!

Answer Anticipation:

This author is dealing with extremes—"If *all* farmers…"; "must not spread *any further*." Surely, there's a middle ground here, where enough food can still be grown even with a higher number of organic farms.

Correct Answer: (B)

Answer Choice Explanations:

A. The author here concedes that farming with artificial fertilizers is damaging to the environment, but she argues that feeding everyone is a more important consideration. There's no balance of how damaging this type of farming is, just that the alternative is much worse.
B. This answer plays into the middle ground possibility—if enough farmers skip enough organic farming, the world can be fed with doing less damage to the environment.
C. At some point in human history, we lived in caves and hunted sabretooth tigers for food. Things change, so this answer has to bearing on the current state of affairs.
D. Close, but the introductory clause of this answer makes it the opposite of what we want. The author assumes that there will be a food shortage if there's any further spread of organic farming; she doesn't overlook that possibility.
E. Similar to (A), the author concedes that using artificial fertilizer is bad, though this answer takes it a step further to connect that to human health. Putting that problem with this answer aside, even if artificial fertilizer is bad for human health, the author could still believe that it's a risk worth taking so people don't starve to death.

Key Takeaway:

In many questions that have strong moral implications (here, environmental sustainability vs. mass starvation), the LSAT will try to get you to pick an answer that makes judgments about those moral questions. Here, (A) and (E) are both trying to play off those moral judgments. Don't fall for the trap! Stick to the argument.

Q22

Argument or Facts: Facts
Valid or Flawed: N/A
Question Type: Must Be True

Stimulus Summary:

Ouch! Motor nerves die when severed, but they regrow slowly and at a set rate. To do so, they need the nerve sheath. This sheath disintegrates within a few months without living tissue in it.

Answer Anticipation:

There's a lot of overlap between these statements, so any anticipation here would be as likely to be a complete miss as something that is close to the correct answer. It's more important in this case to understand the statements and not get confused by the scientific language.

Correct Answer: (D)

Answer Choice Explanations:

A. The success is related to the survival of the nerve sheath, which depends on the presence of living tissue, not the speed of the nerve growth. If a motor nerve is severed 100 mm from the muscle it controls, it doesn't matter if the speed of regrowth is 1 mm or 2 mm, unless something keeps the intervening tissue alive.

B. There's nothing to indicate that the disintegration of a nerve sheath can be reversed. Living tissue can prevent it from disintegrating, but prevention isn't the same as reversing.

C. If living tissue is in the sheath, the three-month deadline doesn't seem to apply. Also, assuming there is no living tissue, the nerve sheath will start to disintegrate and the nerve cell won't regenerate, but if you're going to law school, you probably don't have a medical degree and don't know if there's another way to restore motor function!

D. First off, this answer is very weak, making it easier to support. For example, the last section states this answer only must be true in some cases for it to be supported. Additionally, we are told that living tissue will keep the nerve sheath alive past three months, making it at least possible for the motor nerve to regenerate, which is a higher possibility than 0%.

E. Surgical intervention? Again, if you don't have a medical degree, you don't know what's needed to keep that nerve sheath alive. Maybe some gingko biloba will keep the tissue alive.

Key Takeaway:

When a Must Be True question doesn't ask for absolute certainty (e.g., *most strongly supported*), the correct answer will frequently use very weak language. Additionally, get rid of answers that bring in ideas not mentioned by the author.

Q23

Stimulus Summary:

Adult male dolphins carry sea junk. Researchers thought it was just for fun, but if that were true, then baby and female dolphins would also do it. They don't, so it's more likely a mating display.

Answer Anticipation:

An abstract version of this argument:

If a certain explanation (fun) for a phenomenon (adult male dolphins carrying sea junk) were correct, then another phenomenon (baby and female dolphins carrying sea junk) would also be seen. That phenomenon isn't seen, so another explanation (mating display) is more likely.

Or, even more abstract, if A were true, we'd see B. We don't see B, so probably something other than A.

Correct Answer: (D)

Answer Choice Explanations:

A. If A were true, we'd see B. But not A... As soon as this answer negates the sufficient condition, it can be eliminated for not matching up.

B. A, and if A, then B. This answer can be eliminated after we see that the first sentence triggers the conditional in the second sentence, instead of negating the necessary condition.

C. If A, then B. B... As soon as the necessary condition from the conditional is given instead of negated, this answer can be eliminated.

D. If A, then B. Not B, so probably not A. This answer isn't a direct match to the stimulus because it concludes probably not A, instead of probably something other than A, but it follows the general structure. After eliminating (E), it becomes clear this answer best matches the structure of the given argument.

E. If A, then B. Probably A... As soon as the sufficient condition is given (even as a probability), this answer can be eliminated for not following the same structure as the given argument.

Key Takeaway:

When there's conditional language in a Parallel Reasoning question, diagram the argument using conditional notation to see the structure that the correct answer must follow.

Q24

Argument or Facts: Argument
Valid or Flawed: Valid
Question Type: Methods of Reasoning

Stimulus Summary:

One of Warhol's pieces of art is identical to a stack of Brillo boxes. Therefore, appearance isn't the only consideration in defining a piece of art.

Answer Anticipation:

This argument considers a specific example (*Brillo Boxes* vs. Brillo boxes) to prove a point. It also rules out one possibility (that appearance determines art) through that example, to conclude that something else must matter. Those are two common forms of reasoning, but the correct answer could phrase this in any number of ways, so it's important to stay flexible.

Correct Answer: (E)

Answer Choice Explanations:

A. First, this argument highlights the identical nature of two things, not their differences. Second, it doesn't bring up something believed to have a quality and something that *actually* has that quality—the entire argument is about things believed to be and not to be art.

B. There is an implied opposing argument, concluding that appearance determines art. However, the author here uses a counterexample to disprove that conclusion, not to point out an ambiguity in that argument.

C. The argument does almost the opposite in concluding that one set of boxes is considered art and the other isn't. Additionally, the argument states that the two sets of boxes are *visually* indistinguishable, not actually indistinguishable.

D. There is an implied theory—appearance alone determines art. However, it's just a theory, not an argument, so it would be hard for the author to question the theory's assumptions without explicitly calling them out. Here, the author uses a counterexample to discount that implied theory.

E. Difficult answer! It'd be near impossible to prephrase this answer as stated. However, with the rest of the answer choices ruled out, let's unpack this one. The thesis in question is that appearance alone determines whether something is considered art. If that thesis were correct, then two visually identical things would either both be art or not art. The Warhol example, therefore, would be impossible if the thesis were true, but the Warhol example is itself true, disproving the thesis. Convoluted, but correct!

Key Takeaway:

The correct answer to a Methods of Reasoning question can sometimes be abstract and convoluted. If you encounter an answer like that early on, defer and come back after making some eliminations. When it's time to consider those answers, slow down and unpack it one piece at a time.

Q25

Argument or Facts: **Argument**
Valid or Flawed: **Flawed**
Question Type: **Flawed Parallel Reasoning**

Stimulus Summary:

If both H and S supported a proposal, it would have passed. S claims she supported it. It didn't pass. Therefore, H is a liar.

Answer Anticipation:

The premises do allow for a valid conclusion to be drawn—that someone is lying about their support. However, the author concludes that H is the liar. There's just as much evidence that S is the one lying! The correct answer will similarly establish that one of two things must be true, and then erroneously select one as true instead of validly concluding that either could be true.

Correct Answer: (A)

Answer Choice Explanations:

A. This argument establishes that two things can't be true at the same time—the accident occurred on Aylmer Street, and Morgan witnessed the accident from his kitchen window. So either the TV news (reporting that the accident happened on Aylmer Street) or the newspaper (reporting that Morgan witnessed the accident from his kitchen window) must be wrong. Then, the author picks one of those as being true, without evidence, matching the error in reasoning of the given argument.

   This was a tough answer—the writer of this question did a great job of burying the same flaw in a dissimilar structure!

B. This answer choice doesn't establish two things must be false and then pick one as being the truth.

C. Since the conclusion here deals with the truth of the statements (if Galindo is correct), it doesn't match an argument that erroneously assumes and concludes one of the two options is correct.

D. While this answer assumes that the beliefs of a group are true, it doesn't do so at the expense of a different belief. For this answer to match the given argument, it would have to state that Harris believes she doesn't favor these interests, thus setting up a situation where only one of two options can be correct.

E. This answer doesn't establish that one of two statements must be false. Instead, it *assumes* that two statements couldn't both be true at the same time, overlooking the possibility that unemployment could decrease overall while increasing in a certain segment of the workforce. Contrast that to the given argument, where based on the proposal's failure, it's certain that one of the two individuals definitively didn't support the proposal.

Key Takeaway:

For Flawed Parallel Reasoning, focus on the flaw, not the structure. While arguments that commit the same flaw tend to have similar structures, there are times where that won't be the case, such as here.

PT 86 - LR 2
QUESTION EXPLANATIONS

25 QUESTIONS

In this section we look at each LR question in depth by examining the stimulus, answer anticipation and each answer choice.

Q1

Argument or Facts:	**Argument**
Valid or Flawed:	**Flawed**
Question Type:	**Main Point**

Stimulus Summary:

There's a belief, but it must be mistaken, because a counterexample exists.

Answer Anticipation:

The word *But* indicates a shift, usually from the counterpoint to the author's argument. Here, the author pivots to an assessment of the opposing point, mainly that it's mistaken. When the author gives their opinion of the validity or correctness of a different viewpoint, it's almost always the main point of the argument. Here, the argument goes on to offer a counterexample, which will almost always serve as a premise.

Since the author uses a word to refer back to an earlier idea in the conclusion (this), our prephrase should include that earlier idea. So let's look for *The belief that England's mild winters are due to the Gulf Stream is wrong.*

Correct Answer: (B)

Answer Choice Explanations:

A. This answer is the opposing point. It's rare to get a conclusion about what is *widely believed*.
B. Almost exactly the prephrase!
C. A concession the author makes before introducing her counterexample, not the main point. In the given argument, this clause is introduced with *While*, which is an indicator the author is agreeing with the opposing point, or bringing up a point that is true but doesn't undermine her conclusion.
D. A fact used as a premise/counterexample to the counterpoint.
E. Another fact used as the other half of the premise/counterexample.

Key Takeaway:

When the author pivots to her view of the opposing point, it's almost certain to serve as the main point of the argument.

Q2

Argument or Facts: **Argument**
Valid or Flawed: **Flawed**
Question Type: **Point at Issue**

Stimulus Summary:

E: Anesthesia is pretty safe these days, so nurses with special training should be allowed to give it.

J: These nurses do receive great training, but rare emergencies require a doctor.

Answer Anticipation:

E and J seem to agree the nurses can receive good training, and that anesthesia is relatively safe (J implies it by stating emergencies are rare). However, E thinks the nurses should be allowed to administer anesthesia without a doctor around, whereas J doesn't. Since that's the only point at issue, it should be the correct answer.

Correct Answer: (E)

Answer Choice Explanations:

A. A tempting answer, but a little too extreme! E thinks nurses should be allowed to anesthetize patients, so he'd agree with this sentence. J doesn't think they should be allowed to anesthetize patients *without doctor's supervision*, though, so we can't commit her to disagreeing with this statement.
B. J seems to agree with this statement, but E never discusses emergencies or how rare they are.
C. Both E and J agree that there are nurses with specialized training, but we don't know if they think they should receive *more* training. Neither has a clear opinion here.
D. E agrees with this, but J never speaks to improvements in safety.
E. E disagrees directly with this. J, in stating that *only* doctors have the training to handle emergencies is committed to agreeing with this statement. If doctors are required for the rare emergency, then they should always be supervising the administration of any anesthesia.

Key Takeaway:

For Point at Issue questions, it's often helpful to identify areas of agreement so that those answers can be quickly eliminated.

Stimulus Summary:

Most people rarely look at cigarette packaging. A new law requires packaging to have a bunch of warnings. Therefore, most people will keep smoking.

Answer Anticipation:

For Sufficient Assumption questions, the author will frequently jump from an idea in the premise to a completely different one in the conclusion. Our job is to connect those two ideas.

Here, the author concludes that people will not change their smoking habits since they won't look at the packaging. That's not established by the argument. While that might seem like a solid jump to you, and you may be asking now how could smoking habits be impacted by warnings that people aren't looking at, that's not your job in a Sufficient Assumption question. Instead, we just need to connect the ideas.

Here, let's look for an answer similar to, "If people rarely look at the warnings on cigarette packages, those warnings won't affect their smoking habits."

Correct Answer: (D)

Answer Choice Explanations:

A. Correct Sufficient Assumption answer choices will generally stick to connecting ideas already in the given argument. Here, the answer strays to discussing what should happen, which is outside the scope of the argument.

B. This answer is the inverse of the correct answer. The given premise is about people who rarely look at the packaging, so an answer that has a sufficient condition referencing those who do look at the packaging can't be triggered by the facts established in this argument.

C. While this answer provides a potential explanation as to why the warnings won't impact smoking habits, it doesn't guarantee it. The argument would still need a connection between these people and a failure to change smoking habits.

D. A complicated conditional statement, but this would translate to: If people don't regularly look at the packaging, then the new packaging cannot affect their smoking habits. That conditional connects the argument's premise to its conclusion, and thus it serves as a sufficient condition.

E. This answer doesn't deal with the packaging specifically, or smoking habits at all. Without that, it can't serve as a sufficient assumption to a question that's about the connection between those two.

Key Takeaway:

For Sufficient Assumption questions, stick to answers that connect ideas already present in the given argument.

Stimulus Summary:

W: Before, competitive swimmers were students. Now, they're graduates. Training regimens must have improved.

Y: No, it could be that now swimmers can make a living swimming, whereas they used to need to get a job.

Answer Anticipation:

Warner settles on one potential explanation for a given change, and Young gives another potential explanation. Let's look for an answer that aligns with that view.

Correct Answer: (E)

Answer Choice Explanations:

A. Young provides a different explanation for the same phenomenon Warner has noticed, but she doesn't try to argue that Warner's premise in some way weakens or contradicts his conclusion, which is what we'd need to see for this answer to be correct.

B. The evidence Warner uses is that more and more competitive swimmers have graduated from school. Young, in offering an alternative explanation for that phenomenon, relies on it being true. So Young doesn't undermine Warner's evidence; she agrees with it. This answer would be correct if Young offered examples of all the swimmers who were still in school.

C. Neither Warner nor Young deals in sufficient or necessary conditions, so this answer should be eliminated immediately.E agrees with this, but J never speaks to improvements in safety.

D. This answer is the same as saying Young accuses Warner of making a circular argument. In no way does Young say Warner's premise assumes the truth of the conclusion; in fact, she states that there's a consideration Warner is missing.

E. Warner and Young agree that more and more competitive swimmers have graduated from school. They disagree on why that is (training vs. money). This answer hits at that disagreement.

Key Takeaway:

Alternative explanations, solutions, and causes are all very important on the LSAT. If you can view an argument or statement through one of those lenses, it will probably help you to find the correct answer.

Q5

Stimulus Summary:

B and C are the only qualified applicants. B isn't a team player, so we should hire C.

Answer Anticipation:

There are two options. One has a flaw, so we should pick the other.

Correct Answer: (B)

Answer Choice Explanations:

A. This answer doesn't select between the two offered options, so it doesn't parallel an argument that does.
B. Two options are given; one is mentioned as having problems associated with it. The other is selected, so we should select this answer!
C. This answer doesn't select between the two offered options, so it doesn't parallel an argument that does.
D. This answer has two options, but it selects both of them! That doesn't parallel an argument that selects one of the given options.
E. This answer has two options, and then selects one... first, and the other second. Without that last clause about visiting Peru later, it would be a much better answer.

Key Takeaway:

This Parallel Reasoning question uses a common Method of Reasoning—eliminating alternatives. While different question types generally have different strategies, concepts that show up in one question type will frequently show up in others. When you start noticing that, you'll know your LSAT mastery is nearly complete.

Argument or Facts:	Argument
Valid or Flawed:	Valid
Question Type:	Argument Structure

Stimulus Summary:

Babies can recognize that a three-eyed human is weird, but they can't speak. *They must be thinking in images*, and therefore thinking can occur without language.

Answer Anticipation:

The first statement is a conclusion backed up by research, but the last statement is also a conclusion backed up by the situations described in the research (after all, it starts with *Thus*). When there are two conclusions, we need to figure out which is the main conclusion, and which one supports it. Here, the example of babies thinking about faces supports the more general conclusion about thought occurring without language, so the statement in question is a subsidiary conclusion.

Correct Answer: (A)

Answer Choice Explanations:

A. Exactly right! The research proved a specific conclusion about the way babies think, and it uses that specific conclusion to draw a general conclusion about thinking and language.

B. While the researchers carried out the research, the conclusion of it isn't attributed to those researchers. It's possible the researchers did the study, but the Psychologist is the one drawing the last statement as a conclusion.

C. This is a tempting trap answer, but spending time figuring out which conclusion is the main point and which is subsidiary allows us to avoid it.

D. There is no refutation of the claim that infants have no knowledge of language. In fact, the whole argument rests on infants lacking knowledge of language.

E. A conclusion of research can't be the hypothesis of that research.

Key Takeaway:

When faced with two conclusions in an argument, spend time figuring out which serves as support for the other. In an Argument Structure question with two conclusions, you can expect a trap answer dealing with the difference the main point and subsidiary conclusion.

Q7

Stimulus Summary:

This is a weird stimulus, in that it has an argument and a recommendation, but they're not intertwined by anything other than topics.

The argument is that bones thicken when exercised, so exercise is essential to preventing osteoporosis.

The view is that a diet to prevent osteoporosis isn't high in calcium, but rather low in protein, meat, and dairy, and high in fruits and vegetables.

Answer Anticipation:

Answers that support a causal connection between exercise and bone strength will support the argument. Answers that connect fruits/veggies to strong bones and protein/dairy/calcium to weak bones will support the view.

Correct Answer: (B)

Answer Choice Explanations:

A. This answer supports the argument. It shows an example of missing a given cause (exercise) and missing a given effect (strong bones), thus strengthening that connection.
B. The diet mentioned in the argument is called "essential" for the prevention of osteoporosis. If there are medical therapies that prevent the condition but don't involve a special diet, that would completely undermine the Nutritionist's view. Since it weakens the argument, it serves as a correct answer here.
C. This answer gives an example of the cause (low protein diet) and the effect (no osteoporosis) going together, thus strengthening the claimed causal relationship.
D. This answer supports the author's view that a high-calcium diet won't prevent osteoporosis by giving an example of a population where that connection holds.
E. Another answer which connects the diet recommended by the Nutritionist to the desired outcome—fruits/vegetables and low protein to no osteoporosis.

Key Takeaway:

When being tasked with strengthening a causal argument, look for answers that provide examples of the stated cause and effect both being present or absent.

Q8

Argument or Facts:	Facts
Valid or Flawed:	N/A
Question Type:	Cannot Be Truet (Principle)

Stimulus Summary:

A farm wants to test its cattle for export. However, the government prohibited it because there's no evidence the meat is dangerous enough to warrant scaring the public into thinking it needs to be tested.

Answer Anticipation:

Since the question stem asks us about the government's actions, we should focus there. Here, the government prohibited something because the risk wasn't worth the cost (panic). The correct answer will run at odds to these facts, probably stating something about the government not being justified in prohibiting testing.

Correct Answer: (A)

Answer Choice Explanations:

A. A mouthful! The first half of this answer is a misdirect that doesn't apply to this question since the government in question isn't requiring testing (that's the country to which the beef is being exported). However, the second half of the answer would apply here, and since the government in this question is prohibiting a test, this answer which states a government isn't justified in prohibiting a test runs counter to the prohibition.

B. If anything, this answer aligns with the actions of the government, as they determined whether the testing was warranted and let the company know that it wasn't.

C. This answer aligns almost exactly with the situation, and we're looking for an answer that doesn't.

D. This answer doesn't align with the situation described because there's no indication that the government is paying for the test. Since it doesn't apply, the prohibition can't be at odds with this statement.

E. There were two governments in the stimulus— the government from the importing country, and the government from the exporting country. The question is about the latter, but this answer is about the actions of the former, so it doesn't apply.

Key Takeaway:

Be sure to read an answer choice all the way through. There are many examples of the LSAT including a misdirect in the first half of a correct answer to get you to eliminate it ahead of shifting to the language that makes the answer correct.

Stimulus Summary:

Each vacation lets a worker recharge. Therefore, a larger number of shorter vacations is better than a smaller number of long vacations, if reducing exhaustion is the goal.

Answer Anticipation:

The conclusion here considers two options and picks one over the other. It also establishes a goal—reducing exhaustion. The premise establishes that each vacation reduces psychological exhaustion, but it doesn't state that any length vacation has the same amount of "recharge" to it.

Since the conclusion is about vacations of varying length, but the premise doesn't address how length of vacation impacts charge, there's a jump made by the author. The correct answer will probably bring up that the author overlooks the possibility that a longer vacation might provide a much bigger and longer lasting benefit than shorter vacations.

Correct Answer: (E)

Answer Choice Explanations:

A. The argument assumes that the benefits of short and long vacations are the same, not that each short vacation is the same. The author's argument is still works if short vacations have varying benefits, as long as those benefits are at least as big as the benefit of a longer vacation.

B. The argument deals with a vacation strategy that will maximize psychological benefits, but it doesn't state that nothing else will factor into minimizing exhaustion. For this answer to be correct, the conclusion would have to state that anyone taking many shorter vacations will minimize psychological exhaustion, not that it's what they should do to achieve that effect.

C. Even if different workers may get a different benefit from the short vacations, it could be the case that they all still get a greater benefit from this strategy than taking fewer, longer vacation. If this answer had stated that the benefits of short vs. long vacations differed substantially between workers, then it'd be closer to a correct answer.

D. While total time off may be more important than the number of vacations, each worker only has a set number of days off. This argument is about how to split up those available vacation days, not how many days they receive to begin with.

E. The only answer left, and, luckily, the correct one. This answer points out that, while both short and long vacations may have the same general benefit, the scale of the psychological benefits on long vacations could outweigh the more frequent benefits that would come from the smaller vacations. If someone who takes a week off recharges for 6 months, but someone who takes 3 days off only recharges for a week, the longer vacations would have the larger psychological benefit.

Key Takeaway:

When a conclusion picks an option to the exclusion of another, the correct answer will generally bring up a difference (or similarity, depending on the question type) of the two options.

Q10

Stimulus Summary:

A cave painting in Spain was created 40,800 years ago. Therefore, it's likely by a Neanderthal. Therefore, Neanderthals could think symbolically.

Answer Anticipation:

In a Necessary Assumption question with an intermediate conclusion, the gap in reasoning can be between the premise and intermediate conclusion, or the premises and the main conclusion.

In this argument, the gap between the premise and intermediate conclusion is that Neanderthals were around and the primary species 40,800 years ago.

The gap between the premises and main conclusion is that the creation of a cave painting is evidence of symbolic thought.

We'll have to stay flexible, as either answer could be correct!

Correct Answer: (C)

Answer Choice Explanations:

A. A tempting answer, but a subtle shift here! This answer states that it's *known* that Neanderthals had the manual dexterity to create the cave paintings. The argument doesn't require scientists to have knowledge of that fact; it requires only that the Neanderthals had that ability.

B. Too extreme. While the gap between the premise and intermediate conclusion relates to the primacy of Neanderthals in Spain at the time (in order to connect knowledge of just the time period and location to the likelihood that the paintings are by the Neanderthals), it doesn't require that *no* other hominid species inhabited *any* part of Europe at the time.

C. This answer strikes at the heart of the assumption between the premises and main conclusion. If the ability to create cave paintings doesn't indicate an ability to think symbolically, then the author's argument falls apart, as these paintings are no longer good evidence for the conclusion.

D. This evidence doesn't need to be the first evidence in order to be good evidence. If other evidence already exists, this evidence could still suggest the traditional view is wrong. For this answer to be correct, the conclusion would need to state that this is the first evidence to call the traditional view into question.

E. This answer is the inversion of what the argument needs. We're looking for an answer stating that cave paintings is evidence for symbolic thought, not that a lack of cave paintings is evidence against symbolic thought.

Key Takeaway:

For arguments that have intermediate conclusions, be sure to spot any assumptions between the premise(s) and intermediate conclusion, as well as between the premises (including the intermediate conclusion) and main conclusion.

Q11

Stimulus Summary:

The deadline for a Grant is October 1. It can take 10 days to mail an application from Greendale. Mary, who is mailing her application from Greendale, must mail it out ten days before the due date.

Answer Anticipation:

This argument uses a common misdirect on the LSAT, and it does so through a small word that makes a huge difference.

Since humans tend to focus on nouns, one might read that second sentence as follows: It can take up to TEN DAYS for REGULAR MAIL from GREENDALE to reach GILLESPIE CITY.

However, on the LSAT, logic and certainty are king. Instead, it should be read: It CAN take UP TO ten days for regular mail from Greendale to reach Gillespie City.

That language setting up logic and certainty is easily overlooked on the exam. In this question, the other premise and conclusion use much more certain language (*must, will be, only if*). This jump between the uncertain language of the second sentence and the certain language of the conclusion is an error in reasoning.

Correct Answer: (C)

Answer Choice Explanations:

A. The conclusion of this argument is predicated on Mary sending an application by regular mail from Greendale, so it's not assuming that she does so, it's saying what is true if she does so.

B. The conclusion is predicated on Mary sending in the application by regular mail. If the conclusion was instead, "So if Mary is sending an application by mail from...", then this would be a contender.

C. This answer gets at the discrepancy in certainty that we found. While regular mail can take up to 10 days to get from one location to another, it might not take that long. This answer points out that the 10 days is listed as a potential maximum, not a certain time frame.

D. The entire argument here is about a necessary condition to being considered, and to getting an application in on time (must be, only if). This answer states that the argument assumes getting the application in on time is sufficient for consideration, which the argument never does.

E. Since the entire argument is about regular mail (both premise and conclusion), this answer choice about express mail is out of scope. If anything, the argument is assuming that regular mail is an option as long as you plan it out ahead of time.

Key Takeaway:

Small words on the LSAT sometimes carry a lot of meaning. While the word can is one that most people use almost as a filler in the real world, on the LSAT, it has a specific (and weak) meaning, and when it shows up in an argument, the level of certainty it denotes is usually important to the question.

Q12

Argument or Facts: **Argument**
Valid or Flawed: **Flawed**
Question Type: **Strengthen**

Stimulus Summary:

Hypothesis: The Amazon once flowed into the Pacific, even though it's not blocked off by the Andes and flows into the Atlantic.

Evidence: Freshwater fish that are descendants of extinct saltwater fish from the Pacific (and not Atlantic) live in the Amazon.

Answer Anticipation:

This argument discusses a wide variety of facts (mountains, fish of different types, oceans), so there are a lot of potential answers. Anything that connects the Pacific fish with the Amazonian fish, or rules out those fish coming from the Atlantic, will strengthen the hypothesis.

Correct Answer: (B)

Answer Choice Explanations:

A. The argument specifically states that the fish in the Amazon descended from the Pacific fish, so this answer is out of scope.

B. These fish are the key evidence the author uses to support her conclusion. If the ancestor fish were around before the Andes formed, and the Andes are the blocker in the way of the Amazon going to the Pacific, then that increases the likelihood that, when those fish were still alive, they were able to swim into a non-Andes blocked, Pacific-flowing Amazon.

C. Related to and descended from are different things. Additionally, the fish in question aren't known to be in the Atlantic Ocean at all.

D. Thanks for the geography lesson, LSAT! In any case, this provides context, but the extent of the Andes now doesn't increase the likelihood that, pre-Andes, the Amazon flowed in a different direction.

E. Since the fish in question already made the transition from salt to fresh water, this answer is out of scope.

Key Takeaway:

When an argument throws a variety of facts your way, stay flexible when looking at the answers and consider anything that impacts any of the information from the argument.

Q13

Argument or Facts: **Argument**
Valid or Flawed: **Flawed**
Question Type: Strengthen with Necessary Premise

Stimulus Summary:

Since athletes will do anything for an edge, banning PEDs is futile. If PEDs are given by doctors in safe doses, they're harmless. Therefore, sports leagues should allow doctors to roam around locker rooms, drugging up the athletes.

Answer Anticipation:

The author's making a jump between safe and unavoidable, and a judgment that something should be allowed. The answer will point out some connection between those ideas, but it's hard to anticipate what, exactly, it will state.

Correct Answer: (E)

Answer Choice Explanations:

A. First, the argument cares about inevitability and safety, not respect or harm to the sport. Second, this answer brings up what spectators "know," and the argument doesn't ever give a hint that this information would be public.

B. The argument isn't about fairness, so these drugs having an equal effect on different athletes is out of scope.

C. The Columnist here cares about safety when athletes are going to do something regardless of the legality of it. Taking a drug that has no effect could still be dangerous.

D. The author wants to limit the circumstances under which these drugs are allowed in sports. There is no discussion or assumption about whether doctors are currently the ones providing the PEDs to athletes.

E. Convoluted, but correct! The author states that athletes will take any chance they can to get a competitive advantage, so taking PEDs in inevitable, and the league should make it safe via doctors. If taking PEDs at unsafe levels gives a bigger advantage than taking them at safe levels, then athletes will inevitably do that, and the whole argument breaks down.

Key Takeaway:

Sometimes, recognizing the key ideas is as important as having a specific answer choice anticipation. Especially in Necessary Assumption questions, sometimes a more generic idea of what you're looking for makes it more likely you'll stay flexible enough o find the correct answer.

Q14

Stimulus Summary:

M: Technology is hurting the environment, so humans must go back to a natural way of living.

C: Humans have been using technology to change their environment for thousands of years—*it is natural*—so your criticism is invalid.

Answer Anticipation:

Cora's use of the word *natural* parrots that of Max, so it's probably going to feature in the correct answer. Here, Cora brings up a consideration to refute Max's implication that changing the environment is unnatural.

Correct Answer: (A)

Answer Choice Explanations:

A. Here's our answer. It points out that Cora is rebutting Max's belief that technology is unnatural and hurting the environment (the alleged cause) by showing that it's a part of human nature.
B. Cora and Max aren't debating the relative merits of technology, but rather whether it's natural (and thus whether a return to natural living is a fix).
C. Both Cora and Max agree that technology has been changing the environment; the debate is over whether that's natural.
D. Neither Cora nor Max discusses the difficulty of going back to a more natural way of living. Cora seems to think that we're already living naturally, since using technology is in our nature!
E. Neither argues the morality of technology-driven environmental changes. Even Max just brings up a potential fix, not whether it's a moral one.

Key Takeaway:

When there are two speakers who use the same word, dive in to see if there's a discrepancy in how they're using it, or how they think it applies to the argument. Here, Max and Cora disagree over what counts as "natural," and that helped us find the correct answer.

Q15

Argument or Facts: **Argument**
Valid or Flawed: **Flawed**
Question Type: **Flawed Parallel Reasoning**

Stimulus Summary:

Children haven't gained much weight, on average, over the past 8 years, so the proportion of children who are obese can't have changed much, and therefore the childhood obesity epidemic is a myth.

Answer Anticipation:

Slow down there, Ray Kroc. The argument jumps between the average weight, to a determination about how that weight is spread between the population.
If, over the past 8 years, half the children gained a lot of weight, and the other half got in great shape, the average might stay about the same while the proportion of those who are obese could have shot up.

Correct Answer: (B)

Answer Choice Explanations:

A. This argument jumps between belief and reality. That's a flaw, but it's not the same as the one in the given argument.
B. At this company, it's possible half the employees were fired and replaced with recent college grads earning next to nothing, while the other half gave themselves a nice raise. The average could be about the same, while the number of workers receiving a high salary drastically increased. This is the same error in reasoning.
C. This argument does have a flaw, in that the number of buildings overall could have drastically increased. That's different than the given argument's flaw, dealing with the difference between the average value of something and the distribution of it.
D. This argument deals with a spurious causal assumption, mainly that high-calorie dishes on menus drives weight gain. That's a much different assumption than the one in the given argument.
E. This is a tricky answer, but a good sign that it's incorrect is that the conclusion is about an average, not the premise. This argument's flaw is that it's only considering one possible change—an increase in housing costs—when there is another possibility it doesn't rule out—mainly, that household income has gone down.

Key Takeaway:

The LSAT likes to use averages to trick test takers, since most pre-law students get flustered by anything in the world of math. However, the concept it tests is almost always the same, so revisit a few of these questions to get it down!

Q16

Stimulus Summary:

Kramer is wrong, because the evidence Kramer used to back up his conclusion is wrong.

Answer Anticipation:

Classic error in reasoning. Just because someone makes a bad argument doesn't make them wrong. One could argue that since Die Hard isn't a Christmas movie, it's a good movie. Their premise being wrong (which it is here) doesn't make their conclusion wrong (it isn't here).

If the Editorialist had concluded that Kramer made a bad argument, or his conclusion is invalid, or his conclusion might be false, this would be a valid argument. But the certainty of determining a conclusion is false because the argument behind it has been shown to be bad is a common error in reasoning.

Correct Answer: (E)

Answer Choice Explanations:

A. While the Editorialist does blame Kramer's bad conclusion on the allegation of disgruntled coal miners, she doesn't absolve Kramer of guilt. This answer would be correct if the argument had said that, since one group is guilty, another can't be. That is a flaw—maybe two parties are both guilty—but it's not the flaw here.

B. The argument does conclude a person's statement is false, but it does so based on the argument having shaky facts, not on it impugning the coal industry.

C. The coal miners might have an ulterior motive here, but there's no indication that Kramer does. This ad hominem answer just misses the mark.

D. There's nothing indicating any type of sufficient or necessary conditions here, so this answer, while describing a potential flaw, isn't describing this argument.

E. Perfect answer, and one that you'll potentially see again. This answer describes a common error in reasoning committed on the LSAT—proving an argument is invalid, and concluding that it is false.

Key Takeaway:

When working on Errors in Reasoning questions, it's important to start to notice the repeating errors. If you can start to see these patterns, and the answer choices that describe them, you can increase both timing and accuracy. It can be helpful to keep track of the questions where you note these common errors, and compare arguments that commit the same ones, to hone your ability to spot them, even when they shift topic.

Q17

Stimulus Summary:

Hospitals must protect their patients. The flu is dangerous. Vaccines reduce transmission of the flu. Thus, hospitals must make flu vaccines mandatory for all employees.

Answer Anticipation:

That conclusion is an extreme recommendation. Whenever an argument concludes a recommendation like this, an error in the reasoning is usually that it didn't consider other solutions. For a Necessary Assumption question with an extreme recommendation in the conclusion, the correct answer will usually rule out an alternative. Why? Because if an alternative exists, then the hospital doesn't have to enact this policy, so it's necessary to rule the alternatives out.

Correct Answer: (D)

Answer Choice Explanations:

A. The argument only cares about the protection of the patients, not the rights of the workers. This argument can still be valid even if the employees are mad about the policy.

B. The flu doesn't have to be the *most harmful* threat to patients for a mandatory policy protecting patients from it to be warranted. That would be like saying tarantulas aren't as harmful as rattlesnakes, so no need to worry about those spiders.

C. While this might make it more important to ensure the people under the hospital's control are vaccinated, it doesn't need to be true for the argument to work. Even if only a minority of patients are unvaccinated, it still might be warranted to protect that group by forcing employees to get vaccinated.

D. This answer rules out an alternative policy—a voluntary vaccination policy. If a voluntary policy would be enough to protect patients, then the mandatory one isn't a requirement, and the argument falls apart.

E. What society has accepted doesn't necessarily impact the policies of a hospital. Society hasn't accepted people walking around wearing those hospital gowns, either, but it's still acceptable when you're in the ICU.

Key Takeaway:

Most arguments that make a recommendation in the conclusion do so at the expense of alternative options. Thinking of those alternatives is often the key to success in those questions.

Q18

Stimulus Summary:

Etiquette prevents people from accidentally offending. Etiquette is criticized for being useless to society. Those who criticize it, however, think being nice and getting along is valuable.

Answer Anticipation:

Looking at the overlap between ideas here, it appears as if etiquette helps people get along. That's valuable to the people who criticize etiquette, and it's also an effect of etiquette, so it seems as if these critics are missing the point!

Correct Answer: (C)

Answer Choice Explanations:

A. Tempting answer! However, it states that these critics have contradictory views on etiquette. Their views, as far as we can tell, are internally consistent. They're just wrong about etiquette!

B. There's no indication that any of the critics respect etiquette. They may respect what the author believe etiquette effects, but that's not the same as respecting etiquette itself.

C. Etiquette critics think it's useless. Etiquette critics think being nice is useful. Etiquette helps people be nice. Seems as if the critics are wrong here, and that's what this answer says. It also starts with, "Many people who criticize…", which is a weak answer.

D. First off, it's hard to infer a speculative statement such as this one ("If people were more…"). Second, the author mentions etiquette prevents people from *inadvertently* offending others, which can still happen even if someone is being as considerate as possible. Finally, *no need* is a bit strong.

E. While the critics believe this is true, and the author also appears to agree, it doesn't mean that it's true. If this answer were about what people believed, then it would be correct, but it's about what is true, and there's no support for that in the given facts.

Key Takeaway:

A lot of this question revolved around the ideas of what people believe versus what is true. Especially in a Must Be True question, be careful of jumping between those ideas, as they don't support each other. People can believe things that are false and disbelieve things that are true.

Q19

Argument or Facts: Argument
Valid or Flawed: Flawed
Question Type: Argument Evaluation

Stimulus Summary:

Resin is in wood ant nests. Resin kills deadly ant bacteria. The wood ants probably use resin to protect themselves from disease.

Answer Anticipation:

This is a classic jump between correlation and causation. The author starts with a correlation—resin is in ant nests; resin is a disinfectant. Then, the author states that one of those things motivates (or causes) the other.

Whenever an author selects a motivation, it's suspect, especially when the subject is an animal (did the author interview the ants about their motivations?). Maybe it's just a coincidence that the ants use something that is a disinfectant, but they really use it for another reason. We should be on the lookout for some other reason as we analyze the answer choices.

Correct Answer: (D)

Answer Choice Explanations:

A. Whether the ants get a long or short period of safety from the resin doesn't tell us their motivation behind using it. They could just as easily use it for a short period of safety as a long one.

B. If a premise informed us that the bacteria was more present at certain times of the year rather than others, this answer might be relevant.

C. Other ants may or may not be susceptible to bacteria that is disinfected by the resin. Without knowing that, the answer to this question isn't helpful in analyzing the argument.

D. This answer asks about another potential motivation for using the resin. It's possible the ants use it because it's a good building material, and any disinfectant qualities are merely incidental. If the resin does confer structural benefits, then it hurts the argument that they use it for its disinfectant properties. If it doesn't, then it helps that argument. This is the answer.

E. It doesn't matter how the disinfectant properties came about, just that they did.

Key Takeaway:

For Argument Evaluation questions, it can sometimes be helpful to "answer" the question in the answer choice with Yes and No to see what impact it has on the argument. The correct answer will strengthen the argument with one answer, and weaken it with another.

Q20

Argument or Facts:	Facts
Valid or Flawed:	N/A
Question Type:	Must Be True

Stimulus Summary:

Safe passwords are hard. Easy-to-remember passwords are easy to guess. Safe passwords are hard to remember, and users write them down, making them the most insecure. Forgetting a password takes up time by the system administrator.

Answer Anticipation:

A lot of this question is going to be about simplifying the relatively complex language the given statements use. However, the concepts are luckily ones that most of us live with every day.

The facts given seem to revolve around the pros and cons of passwords that are easy and hard to remember. Throughout the statements, it seems a relatively balanced view, until that last statement, where it's stated that writing down a password is *the greatest security threat of all*. That's an extreme statement, and so it's likely to factor into the answer choice.

Correct Answer: (C)

Answer Choice Explanations:

A. A fiendishly difficult answer choice to eliminate. While the author does state that writing down a password poses the greatest security threat of all, she doesn't make a value judgment about that, so an answer that states what people *should* do is unsupportable.

B. While the author does state that forgetting a password takes up the system administrator's time, there's no indication that that time is expensive. Maybe it's just annoying for the sysadmin!

C. Since difficult-to-remember passwords are generally written down, and that *the greatest* security threat, all other security threats must be less than that. Hence, this answer choice is supported.

D. The random letter/number passwords appear to be the ones that are written down, and are thus the *greatest* security threat, not the least likely to result in a breach.

E. While the takeaway here is that hard-to-remember passwords that are written down are a greater security threat than easy-to-remember ones, it doesn't follow that there's a scale that continues from easiest-to-remember being the most secure to hardest-to-remember being the least secure. "Password" is easier to remember than your anniversary, but the latter is still easy to remember and most likely more secure.

Key Takeaway:

In Must Be True questions, extreme statements often lead to the correct answer. You should perk up when you see one and use it to help you find the correct answer.

Q21

Argument or Facts:	Argument
Valid or Flawed:	Flawed
Question Type:	Main Point

Stimulus Summary:

Since they use waste wood, wood-pellet stoves don't cause trees to be killed; regular wood stoves do cause trees to be killed. So wood-pellet stoves are better for the environment, and if you use a wood stove, it should be a wood-pellet one.

Answer Anticipation:

The first statement in this argument has "should" in it, suggesting it's a conclusion. The final statement starts with "So", also suggesting it's a conclusion. The trick here is to figure out which is the main point and which is a subsidiary conclusion.

To do so, we need to see which one supports the other. Does the recommendation that you should use a wood-pellet stove support that it's better for the environment? Does the wood-pellet stove being better for the environment support the recommendation to use one over a normal stove? The latter makes more sense—a reason to do something supports that course of action—so the first statement is the main point, and what we should look for in the answers.

Note—If you said that there was another intermediate conclusion here (that wood-pellet stoves don't cause additional trees to be killed), you'd be correct! It's supported by the initial clause in that sentence.

Answer Choice Explanations:

A. This is a premise supporting the intermediate conclusion (wood-pellet stoves being more environmentally friendly).
B. The intermediate conclusion! Not only should you avoid this answer, but you should have also anticipated it as a trap answer.
C. Whether you viewed this as another intermediate conclusion, or as a premise of the argument, it's not the main point since it's used to support both the last sentence and, therefore, the main point.
D. This is a premise that allows for the comparison to be made between regular wood stoves and wood-pellet stoves.
E. Here we go! The comparison between the types of stoves leads to the intermediate conclusion that one is more environmentally friendly than the other, building to this main point about which people should use.

Key Takeaway:

When there is an intermediate conclusion (or conclusions, in this case!), be sure to see which supports the other. When a reason is given for a recommendation, the recommendation is almost always the main point, supported by the reason for doing it.

Correct Answer: (E)

Q22

Stimulus Summary:

People would pay much less than the actual cost for gifts selected for them by others, so they clearly value gift cards, which let them select their own gifts, more.

Answer Anticipation:

The premise is about the price a person would pay for an item, and then it jumps to value. While the amount someone would pay for an item is tied to the value, it's not the only thing that determines it. There could be some value in receiving a specific gift from a person even if you wouldn't have bought it yourself. Maybe it gains sentimental value?

Any answer that brings up different ways to define value that suggests a person might value a gift given to them at a higher price than they'd pay for it is in play.

Correct Answer: (D)

Answer Choice Explanations:

A. If anything, this answer strengthens the argument by suggesting people don't value gifts they've received, as they're returning them.

B. This answer is trying to trap you into thinking that gift cards can't be highly valued since if they were, they'd make up a larger percentage of gifts given. However, that's highly speculative and requires several large assumptions, since there's no reason to believe that particularly valuable gifts would be particularly well known, or that there's not another reason people skip giving gift cards (maybe they're highly valued but seen as impersonal).

C. This answer choice would only be in play if it stated that these higher valued gifts exceed the value of the item/gift card. The comparison is out of scope since it doesn't give us enough information to compare the value to the gift cards from the conclusion.

D. This answer suggests that, once a person has received an item as a gift, it becomes more valuable to them. The price someone would sell an item for is at least as valid a measurement as what they'd pay for it, and so this calls into question whether someone would rather receive a gift card. Maybe it really is the thought that counts!

E. While this answer represents an annoyance in returning the gifts, it doesn't necessarily impact the valuation of the gift.

Key Takeaway:

When an argument compares two things, make sure the answer you select necessarily impacts that comparison. Here, even though (D) doesn't mention the gift cards, since those have a value printed on them, knowing of a definitive increase in the value of the gifts impacts the comparison of which is more valuable.

Q23

Argument or Facts: **Argument**
Valid or Flawed: **Flawed**
Question Type: **Weaken**

Stimulus Summary:

A new antitheft device makes it easier to apprehend people after they've stolen a car. In cities where even only a few people are using it, auto theft has dropped a lot.

Answer Anticipation:

The first oddity here is that the device can only help apprehend people after they've stolen a car, not before, so the car thefts are already happening. The second oddity is that it's so effective even with only a few cars equipped with it. What could help explain these paradoxes?

We do know that apprehensions increase drastically with the new device. So people are getting arrested. How could a few arrests drastically lower the overall car theft rate? If getting a few car thieves off the street has a dramatic impact on theft rates, we have our explanation, so let's look for that.

Correct Answer: (E)

Answer Choice Explanations:

A. This answer aligns with the scenario described, in that the new device is hard for even the most experienced thieves to detect. It certainly explains why it increases the odds of apprehending the car thief. However, it doesn't explain the dramatic drop in cities where only a few cars are using the device.
B. By stating that the number of cars stolen in these cities is low, it might explain why car thefts are *low* with just a few devices. However, it still doesn't explain why the number of thefts dropped dramatically after the devices were put into use.
C. This answer aligns with the scenario, but it doesn't explain the precipitous drop in thefts with only a few devices installed. The given scenario already told us that the odds of apprehension are much high*er* with the device; it doesn't really matter if those odds started low or high.
D. This is probably an answer that will trap many students because it sounds good and it's hard to pin down exactly what impact it would have, but it sounds like it would have an impact.
E. Here's our explanation! If a few car thieves steal most of the cars, it wouldn't take many apprehensions before the majority of car thieves were off the streets and thus not stealing cars.

Key Takeaway:

When an answer choice lays out a complex scenario that seems to have an impact on a paradox, walk through the possibilities to see what impact that would be. If there's more than one potential impact depending on assumptions being made, it's safe to say that the answer choice is a trap.

Q24

Stimulus Summary:

Internet: Dense, interconnected, transmits information, growing at millions of points.

Brain: Dense, interconnected, transmits information, growing at millions of points.

So the internet will one day gain humanlike intelligence. And James Cameron will buy the movie rights.

Answer Anticipation:

This argument relies completely on a comparison between two entities. The structure boils down to:

Two things are similar on a few metrics. Therefore, they'll be similar on this other metric.

However, the argument never gives any reason to believe that the similarities it establishes in the premises are the right ones to establish the similarity in the conclusion. Its akin to saying that Ford factories and Pringles factories both have workers and machines, so therefore Pringles will one day turn out automobiles.

Correct Answer: (D)

Answer Choice Explanations:

A. While the argument does use the complexity as a point of similarity between the internet and the brain, it doesn't then go to say that that's the same thing as intelligence. In fact, it says that complexity plus a few other things will lead to intelligence, thus drawing a separation between the two.

B. The conclusion just states that the internet will become intelligent, not that it will be the first technology to do so.

C. While the argument does draw this analogy, there's no reason to think it's a dubious one. If this answer gave a reason to believe it was dubious, then we'd have to consider it deeper, but it doesn't, so we have no reason to question the analogy.

D. The argument draws a few comparisons between brains and the internet, and then goes on to state that they'll become similar in another way. There's no premise stating what makes the brain intelligent, though, and this answer points that out. It uses sufficient language, which we didn't anticipate, but it still gets at the same ideas. If the argument established that the listed elements made the brain intelligent, then it'd be on stronger footing.

E. The argument doesn't care about intentions. It's possible that the internet becomes intelligent without the administrators intending it. In fact, that's the premise of essentially every sci-fi film of the 90s!

Key Takeaway:

Just because two things are similar in many ways doesn't mean they'll be similar in any other ways. When an argument is comparing two things, know that the comparison doesn't necessarily extend past the comparisons drawn in the premises.

Q25

Argument or Facts:	Argument
Valid or Flawed:	Flawed
Question Type:	Strengthen

Stimulus Summary:

Income inequality and immobility lead to divisive political factions and bad governance, which are bad for democracy. Economic expansion increases opportunity for economic mobility. Therefore, democratic societies should promote economic expansion constantly.

Answer Anticipation:

The argument establishes income inequality and immobility as bad for democracy. It then states one method of supposedly alleviating these problems: economic expansion.

There are two issues here. First, maybe the opportunities available through economic expansion make the problem worse. If the opportunities all accrue to the rich and middle class, that could make income inequality worse. Second, maybe there are some other impacts not stated in the stimulus that would lead to worse outcomes for democracy.

Any answer that rules out one of these two issues (or provides another reason that economic expansion is good for democracy) would serve to strengthen this argument.

Correct Answer: (C)

Answer Choice Explanations:

A. This answer strengthens an argument that it's important to address these issues, since they're in a positive feedback loop, but it doesn't strengthen the argument that we should do so through this particular method.
B. This answer increases the political feasibility of the method suggested, but it doesn't strengthen the argument that it's the right method. The politically easiest solution is quite often the wrong move!
C. If economic opportunities from economic expansion disproportionately benefit those at lower income levels, then income inequality will shrink, and the argument states income inequality is bad for democracy. That strengthens an argument in favor of economic expansion (and it lines up with our first anticipation)..
D. Rephrasing this answer, it states that investments by the 1% are a necessary condition for economic expansion. Listing requirements for a solution—whether they are hard or easy to achieve—doesn't impact an argument about whether a solution is what should be done, unless the argument itself is comparing different methods and states that "ease of use" is a relevant factor. That doesn't happen here, so this answer can be ruled out.
E. First, this answer is very weak—can be an obstacle—which makes it harder to have an impact on the argument. Second, even if these parties are an obstacle to economic expansion, that doesn't rule that expansion out as a potential solution to the problems facing a democracy. If anything, it means the solutions should be focused on faster!

Key Takeaway:

Problems, solutions, and author recommendations are a recurring and important feature on the LSAT. When you see an argument structured around these things, focus on the author's solution and why the author thinks it will work.

Try The #1-Rated LSAT Prep for Free.

⚡ **Instant & Lifetime Access**

📄 **90 Full Length LSATs**

% **99th Percentile Instructors**

📱 **Authentic Digital LSAT/ LSAT-Flex Experience**

📈 **Detailed Analytics**

🕐 **Weekly Office Hours**

🏅 **Higher Score Guarantee**

🏆 **#1 for 3 Years in a Row**

lsatmax↗

COMPREHENSIVE LSAT PREP ON MOBILE & WEB

Get 10% Off When You Enroll.

Kyle Ryman
Texas A&M

I scored below a 150 on my first practice LSAT in November. **In June I took the LSAT and scored a 170. I couldn't have done it without LSATMax.**

Anita Yandle
University of Washington

The tutorials from LSATMax helped me get my 99th percentile score! It was great to have the videos at my fingertips at all times so that I could study any time I had a moment.

Austin Sheehy
University of Central Oklahoma

LSATMax is my hero! **My starting score was around a 155-158, and I scored a 170 on the June LSAT!**

Naader Banki
USC

I used LSATMax to study for the October LSAT. **I started out with a diagnostic somewhere in the 150s, and improved my score to 166 on the October test.**

To Redeem Visit lsatmax.io/86
or Call (855) 464-9890

Claim your Free 30-Min LSAT Consultation

Ensure a strong start to your LSAT prep. Schedule your free LSAT consultation with a *99th percentile instructor*.

To Redeem Visit
lsatmax.io/consult-86